JEFF GERKE

HA

YOUR

READER'S

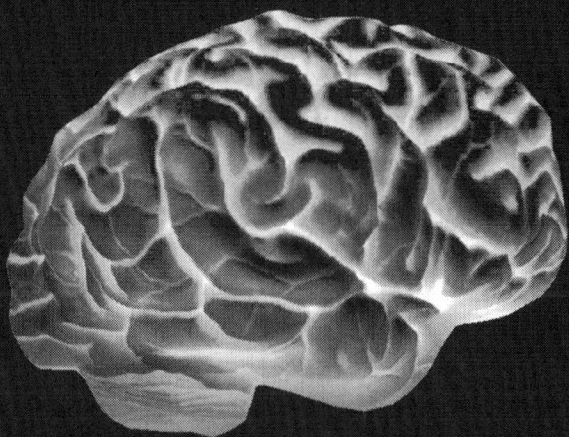

BRAIN

BRING THE POWER OF BRAIN CHEMISTRY

TO BEAR ON YOUR FICTION

Hack Your Reader's Brain by Jeff Gerke

Visit Jeff online at www.jeffgerke.com
See Jeff's digital artwork at art.jeffgerke.com

*Your job as a writer
is to have the reader
become the character.*

Dr. Paul J. Zak, neuroscientist

1

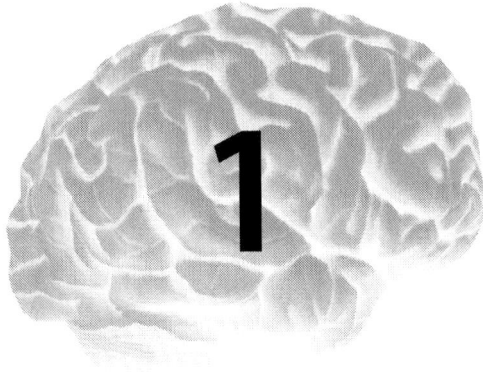

Anatomy of a Bestseller

"You've got to read this novel I just finished—I couldn't put it down!"

Sound good? Would you like readers to say that about the fiction your write? I'm guessing yes.

All of us dream to hear readers say they found our book irresistible, that they consumed it in a single sitting, or that they looked up and realized it was three in the morning and had no idea where eight hours had gone.

We want them reading the last page and then immediately going to Amazon to see if we've written anything else.

Most of all, we want them becoming evangelists for our book, making it their mission to get everyone in their circle to stop what they're doing, hurry to a bookstore, and snag themselves a copy of their own.

Because when lots of people buy lots of copies, that makes a bestseller.

Yes, But How?

Of course we want that, but how do we do it?

Creating a bestseller is a great big ol' mystery . . . or else everyone would be doing it.

What if I told you I could guarantee that you could keep your reader reading your book from beginning to end, even staying up well past bedtime to finish the book?

Can I guarantee a bestseller? 'Fraid not. I wish. But I can guarantee that, if you use the skills I'm going to give you in this little book, you will keep your reader hooked from start to finish. Whether she'll become an evangelist for your book, and whether her evangelism will prove abundantly fruitful, is out of my hands and yours.

But the first part, the crucial part—keeping her glued to the story until "The End"—*is* in our hands.

And I'm going to show you how.

What It Isn't

Not only am I a published novelist and former publisher of a fiction-only publishing house, I also teach writers how to write great fiction.

For the first 20 years of my writing, editing, publishing, and teaching career, up until 2014 or so, I believed that a novel had a chance to become a bestseller if the fiction craftsmanship used in writing it was at a high level. Become a great craftsman, I believed and taught, and your book can take off.

So I spent those 20 years traveling the country and the world teaching the craft of fiction. It was time well spent, and I don't regret a moment of it.

But over the years, I couldn't ignore a certain phenomenon. Time after time, blockbuster novels would light the world on fire, and when I read them, I would find, almost universally, this awful, sickening truth.

The books stunk.

They were terribly written. Awful. Heinous. Atrocious. Scandalously bad.

Not in the stories or themes or characters or whatever, but in the craft. Chapters full of telling. Horrible vocabulary and stupid wordings. Insipid dialogue and archaic speech attributions. The author didn't seem able to keep a consistent POV to save his or her life. Don't get me started about the –ly adverbs, gerunds, and passive voice.

And yet . . .

And yet, they were blockbuster bestsellers.

When I finished teaching any given class at a writers' conference, inevitably someone would come up to me and say, "You just told us to show and not tell [or whatever I'd just spoken on], but [insert name of bestselling novel] is full of telling on every page. How do you explain that?"

My answer was usually something like, "That book isn't a bestseller because of all the telling but in spite of it." But even as I said it, I knew it was lame. And after saying it again and again for years, it finally got to me.

What, I asked myself, is going on here? Why *do* books with horrible craftsmanship become bestsellers? Why do these craft issues seem so important to me but seem to have no impact on a book's success?

Is there an *inverse* relationship, I wondered? Do all novels with bad craftsmanship become bestsellers? Is that the secret? Are novels with good craftsmanship somehow turning readers off?

No, that theory didn't work, because some books with high craft actually do become bestsellers, and *many* books with low craft do sink into oblivion.

So what was going on?

It wasn't that novels with high craft did well or poorly, or that novels with low craft did poorly or well. The awful truth that loomed before me was that craft, high or low, *seemed to have no bearing whatsoever on a book's success.*

Think about that. I found it deeply sobering—and sad.

But it seemed to fit the observed facts.

Amazon Comments

How many times have you read a 5-star Amazon review that read like this, "I *loved* this book because there were no to-be verbs!"?

Yeah, I haven't seen that one either.

"I gave this book only three stars because the writer stuck with 'said' and 'asked' instead of using alternatives like 'opined' and 'queried,' and also she used the word 'that' a lot."

Haven't spotted many like that? I don't mean reviews written by the frustrated novelists panning a book for craft issues, but real people, the average reader, the Wal-Mart reader. Those folks like or dislike a book for reasons other than craft.

They don't complain about the sentences that begin with participial phrases—they say they couldn't stop thinking about the story even when they weren't reading.

They don't laud a novel because it doesn't include buried dialogue—they laud it because they couldn't stop turning pages.

They don't bemoan the many characters whose names began with the same letter—they say they felt like they knew the characters and held them almost as friends or family.

Whatever mysterious thing makes a novel a bestseller isn't its use (or non-use) of a prologue or the immediate (or delayed) occurrence of the inciting event. It apparently, to judge by Amazon reviews, has almost nothing to do with the things we concern ourselves with at writers' conferences and in books and articles on improving fiction craftsmanship.

It has less to do with the how, it seems, and more to do with the what. The how is craftsmanship, but the what is *engagement*. Utter, unshakeable, overpowering enthrallment.

So What Have I Been Doing All This Time?

The realization that the fiction craftsmanship I'd spent so long teaching—and upon which I'd built a career—seemed to have little or no effect on whether a book became a bestseller or not was a hard blow to absorb. It took me to the mat, if you want to know the truth.

I felt like the medieval physician who has been bleeding patients and using leechcraft for his entire career, who then comes to believe that everything he's been doing has not been helpful at all. If the patient got better, he realizes, it was in *spite* of his ministrations, not because of them. And how many patients did he lose (i.e., kill) because he'd been operating under the wrong philosophy of medicine?

The issue wasn't so much that his care harmed or helped. The issue was that all his study of humours and balancing phlegm with bile in the choleric patient *had no bearing whatsoever*. His leeches had as much to do with a patient's recovery as a tuna fish has to do with the shape of a snowflake.

I can imagine him throwing his hands up in despair and crying, "What have I been *doing* all this time? I need to stop getting in the way of the patient's health and see if I can figure out what I should be doing instead. But if the balance of humours isn't the key to health, what is?"

That's What I Did

When I realized that my own teaching about fiction craftsmanship, while solid, wasn't giving my students or clients much improvement in their book's chances to become bestsellers, I found myself in a crisis. I needed to start teaching things that would help a novel's chances, or I needed to find another line of work.

So I asked myself, if high craft isn't what makes a novel a bestseller, what is?

I went back to that anomaly I'd had to contend with every time anyone had asked me about some bestseller that broke all the rules of craft. That's where the secret seemed to lie. If I could figure out why a book could succeed despite low fiction quality, I would be on to something big.

I turned to Amazon reviews, that great barometer of reader satisfaction. I read the reviews for those blockbusters that were terribly written, weeded out the reviews written by frustrated novelists (always the harshest critics), and examined what was left.

Here's a sampling:

"Jasper captured my heart."

"Suspenseful and really enjoyable."

"A fine bit of fun."

"Couldn't put it down! Read it over a weekend."

"An easy read and a captivating love story."

"A fun adventure with just enough science to make the story plausible."

"A hypnotic reading experience."

"Excellent sci-fi thrills."

"I fell in love with the characters!"

"The book was an alarming cautionary tale."

"AMAZING love story! Just read it!"

"There's humor, there's danger, there's adventure, there's fun—it's all there!"

What About Passive Voice?

In that whole search, one thing I didn't find was a review like this: "I gave the book five stars because it didn't have a prologue." Or, "This book gets only one star because it used floating body parts, described the weather, and used speech attributions other than 'said' or 'asked.'" Or, "Only four stars—it was great but the author used passive voice."

Yeah, not so much.

What finally dawned on me—duh—was that the end user, the reader, doesn't give a flying whoop for gerunds, questions not in dialogue, or use of the word "that," and she wouldn't know a POV error if it bit her on the nose.

She doesn't know what constitutes high fiction craftsmanship, and she doesn't care. In fact, if you were to explain beats, show vs. tell, and agenda-driven fiction to her, she'd probably laugh and ask if you'd ever actually *read* a novel.

And that's just it: It's not the end user of fiction who cares about these issues—it's just us in the middle. Agents, editors, writing teachers, and the serious students of fiction writing.

Bestsellers, it turns out, don't happen because authors impress the literary elite. Bestsellers happen when they please the typical reader.

(Now, impressing the literary elite is often what you have to do to get a book traditionally *published*. But in terms of what floats the end user's boat, it's a whole different set of measures.)

Look back at those Amazon comments about novels the readers loved. Where are the comments about craft? There aren't any, not from typical readers. What's there instead are comments about the fun the reader had, the hypnotism of the love story, the thrilling suspense, and the spellbinding escapism the book provided.

That, my friend, is what your reader wants. That is what makes bestsellers.

What Is "That," Exactly?

In *The Irresistible Novel,* one of my books for Writer's Digest, I examine more than 100 "rules" of fiction that experts disagree on. "Never use –ly adverbs," for instance, or "Never use prologues."

After discussing each one, giving writers the tools they need to get de-paralyzed by these conflicting "rules," I leave them with only one rule: The Great Commandment of Fiction. It's my way of rolling all those "Couldn't stop reading it!" comments into one.

The Great Commandment of Fiction is this: *You must engage your reader from beginning to end.*

It's not actually possible to do all of the 100+ "rules" of fiction correctly, since many of them negate or argue against each other. However, even if it were possible to obey all those rules, you could do so and still not engage your reader. Wouldn't that be a tragedy? To do all that work on craft and it still not amount to more than a hill of beans?

Conversely, if you *do* engage your reader—I mean, well and truly engage the tar out of your reader—you can break all 100+ of those rules and the reader simply won't care. Won't notice and won't care. A reader who loves your book loves your book.

(Again, if you're trying to get traditionally published, you may have to pay attention to some of those rules. Sadly, your book may get rejected by editors and agents if you don't, even though no one outside of publishing cares about those rules. [sigh])

I've read fascinating and compelling fiction in which the author broke rules. Sure, the editor part of my mind registered those violations, but the *reader* part of my brain was so utterly captivated by the story that those things didn't bother me in the least. My brain was getting what it wanted—engagement—and nothing else mattered.

I've also read novels that were technically fine but that just left me flat. Unfortunately, that's often what comes out the other end of the critique group process: a (possibly) technically improved but lifeless book. The author has been nailed on – ly adverbs and said/opined by helpful critique group friends, but whatever might have made the book special and great has been buried under a dump-truck load of rules. (I do know that many critique groups aren't like that.)

Most of the time, people critiquing a novel don't even try to talk about fiction rules unless something isn't working in your book. If it's working—by which I mean that the reader is deeply engaged by it—no one talks about show vs. tell or how much description you've put in. (At least, no one *should* take you to task about those things if the book is working.) It's usually only when the book isn't working that people pull out the rules. "Well, I couldn't quite get into your story. Maybe if you stopped beginning sentences with participial phrases, it would help." Or "Sorry, but my mind wandered in this section. Try swapping *said* with *opined* and see if that helps."

No, when a novel has the reader engaged, you'll most likely hear, "Don't change anything!" or "Honestly, I was so taken by what you'd written that I forgot to write any notes!" from your crit partners. Bravo! That's when we know we've engaged our readers.

If you had to choose between spending ten hours and/or $200 on a class on how to improve your fiction craftsmanship or ten hours and/or $200 on a class on how to make your reader more engaged, I urge you to choose the latter.

You can get all the rules right and still write a non-engaging book that readers put down. Or you can get some (or all) of the rules wrong and write a novel that readers devour and tell all their friends about. Which would you rather have?

Of course, that's a false dichotomy. You can have a novel with high craftsmanship that is also highly engaging. That's the Holy Grail. But you might just consider shifting your attention from gerunds and floating body parts to what actually makes a story engaging to readers.

Don't Be Boring!

Perhaps you've seen this acronym in online discussions: TL;DR. It means, "Too long; didn't read." In other words, someone had written a block of text, but it seemed too dense, too wordy, and just too boring to be worth the reader's time. So he didn't read it.

You don't want your reader saying TL;DR about your fiction, either. If a book feels boring, it becomes a burden, and I don't care if it's only ten pages long, readers aren't going to read it.

You must keep your reader engaged from beginning to end.

That's saying it in a positive way. Keep your reader hooked. Keep her reading. Keep her turning pages. Keep her engrossed.

Now here it is expressed in a negative way:

Don't be boring.

So, yes, let's not be boring. Let's make our novels utterly enthralling from start to finish.

No problem, right? Sure, easy peasy.

Actually, it is.

2

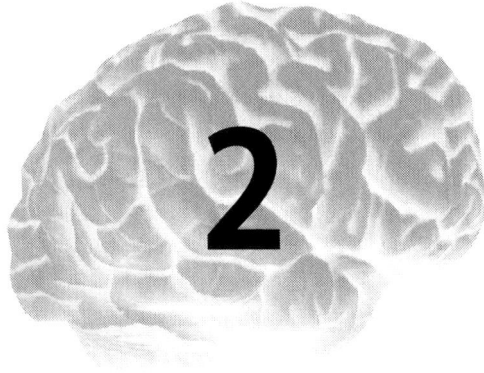

Brain Science to the Rescue

When I realized that neither the rules of fiction nor the craft of fiction was what made a bestseller, and when I hit upon the idea that what *did* make a bestseller was keeping the reader engaged, an obvious question stood before me: How?

How do I engage the reader from beginning to end? How do I keep my fiction from being boring?

I first went back to my Writer's Digest book *The First 50 Pages* to review what I'd written about how to gain the reader's engagement at the beginning of a novel. I saw great material there and I knew it would be helpful. But I wasn't convinced I had the full picture.

I surveyed the rest of my material, both from my teaching notes and from my other books, and collected quite a bit of strong content on how to not only gain the reader's engagement but maintain it throughout the reading experience. But I still didn't feel I had anything really revolutionary. And revolutionary was what I needed.

Enter the Good Dr. Zak

While I was collecting this material, I ran across an article about a scientific study measuring viewer engagement and a neurotransmitter called *oxytocin.*

The study, run by neuroscientist Dr. Paul J. Zak of Loma Linda University, looked at people watching a test video, and it used a number of methods to measure whether they were engaged by the video or not.

Blood draws were taken before showing the video, and also after, for comparison. Participants were fitted with functional magnetic resonance imaging (fMRI) sensors while the video was shown. And after the video, participants were given a survey about how willing they were to contribute to children's cancer research.

In the first part of the test, Dr. Zak and his team showed the participants a short video of a father and his two-year-old son walking at the zoo. That was pretty much all: just walking.

You might be able to guess the results found by the testing measures. The levels and mix of neurotransmitters in the blood after the video were almost exactly the same as before the video. The fMRI showed the viewers' brains barely registering any activity beyond just maintaining a waking state. And the survey at the end showed negligible interest in contributing to cancer research.

But in the second part of the test, Dr. Zak's participants were shown a similar video of a man and his son, but this time, the narrator explains that the little boy is dying of cancer. Indeed, he has only months left to live. He's so young, the parents haven't told him of his condition. The father is deeply grieving but hides his sorrow to give his son perhaps his last day of joy.

What do you think the measures showed this time? The "after" blood draw revealed vast quantities of oxytocin, the neurotransmitter released when we feel *empathy*. The fMRI showed participants' brains lighting up with engagement and activity. And the survey showed a very high willingness to contribute to children's cancer research.

Don't miss the crucial point here: With the use of a made-up story, researchers were able to *change the brain chemistry* of the participants. After the video, those people felt differently, thought differently, and behaved differently.

The researchers had used fiction to hack their brains.

Let's You and Me Do That Too

When I read the article about that study, I knew I'd found the revolutionary material I'd been looking for. If bestsellers happen only when a novel keeps the reader engaged from beginning to end, and if this researcher had figured out how to tap into people's brains to basically *force* them to be and stay engaged, then his findings were essential for me to take hold of.

So I tracked down Dr. Paul J. Zak and told him what I was doing. He was interested in applying his findings to fiction, so he agreed to help me out. We collaborated on Part 2 of *The Irresistible Novel,* and now I'm bringing that information to you.

From Dr. Zak, I learned a great deal about using brain science to gain and hold the brain's attention. I have adapted these to show you how to gain and hold *reader* engagement from beginning to end. Here are the four elements:

1. Catching the reader's attention at the beginning of your novel
2. Securing reader engagement in Act 1
3. Increasing reader engagement through Act 2
4. Fulfilling reader engagement in Act 3

And that, by a crazy, random happenstance, represents more or less the table of contents for the rest of this book.

Let's hack your reader's brain.

3

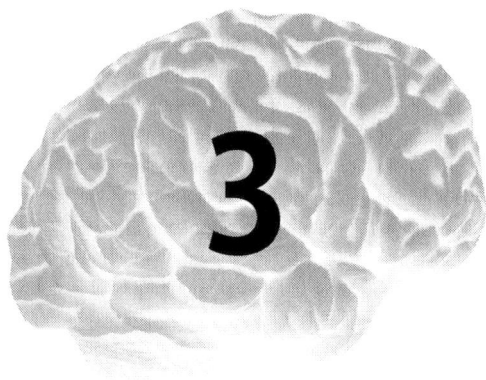

Catching the Reader's Attention

How many pages will you read of a novel that doesn't catch your attention? Assuming your sister didn't write it and you're not being paid to read it, if it's a snooze at the beginning, and you're reading for fun, how many pages will you give it if it *isn't* any fun?

Most readers wouldn't be able to articulate it, but they come to fiction to be entertained. Swept away. Transported. They want to get caught up in a story with fascinating characters and nail-biting suspense. They're hoping you'll give them the things they rave about in Amazon reviews.

Which is to say, they want to be engaged. As in, not disengaged. Not bored. And if your book doesn't engage them, they'll go find one that will.

This means you must engage readers right away. Like on page 1. *Line* 1.

You must catch your reader's attention. I don't care what other wonderful material you've included in your book, if you don't convince your reader right away that this is something she must pay attention to, you're lost, and the reader will never get to enjoy the wonders you've prepared for her later in the book. We can't let that happen.

Happily, you can take advantage of the way the brain works to be absolutely certain you will catch the reader's attention.

Doesn't that sound nice? How many times do we write something and *hope* it will be effective? How many times do we use a technique that someone says has been powerful with some readers but we have no guarantee if it will work for our readers? It's amazing to be able to use a technique with lab science results behind it. It takes the guesswork out of reader engagement.

Hacking the Reader's Attention Through Danger

If there's one thing the brain is constantly scanning for, it's danger. Peril. Impending harm to life or limb.

If you're sitting somewhere reading this book but then a fire breaks out right beside you, your brain is going to prioritize your safety over your edification. You won't be able to help it: You'll pay attention to the fire—assessing the danger, moving to safety—until it's no longer a true danger. At that point, your brain may allow you to go back to reading.

It is one of the beautiful oddities of the human brain that it can experience things *vicariously.* If you're in danger, you feel it and your body reacts to get you to safety. But it's also true that if someone *tells* you about danger they were in, or you watch it on TV, you can begin feeling something of that same danger yourself. As if you were in the danger. That's why, when someone relates a harrowing story, we can't *not* listen.

Be sure to notice that part of it: Even if you're just hearing about a story that happens to someone else, your body and brain can react as if the events are happening to you.

We can use this beautiful oddity to our advantage as novelists.

If you depict a character in danger, your reader will pay attention. Guaranteed. The attentional circuits will fire, telling her to give heed to these matters. She won't be able to not pay attention.

It's almost not fair how well this works.

Ever heard a fiction teacher say, "Begin with action"? Now you know the brain science behind why that works.

If you write a scene in which a cobra slithers into a bank of tall African grass and then you show a toddler chasing a ball toward that grass, your reader will pay attention. Rapt attention. Will the baby be okay?

But why? It's just ink on a page (or electrons on a screen)—how can it possibly have the power to control the behavior and attention of an otherwise autonomous adult? Neuroscience, baby.

It doesn't have to be just physical danger, by the way. Emotional danger or psychological risk work just as well. If you write a scene in which a teen girl goes to a dance party with a boy who thinks she's wonderful, and then a boy she knew at her previous school—who knew all about the reputation she's trying to leave behind—arrives unexpectedly and is surely going to spot her and undo the new life she's building for herself, so she jumps behind a large fern as he nears . . . your reader will read and read until you get her out of that pickle.

We can't help it. We're wired to pay attention to danger. And if it's someone else's danger, that's almost better. We get to feel a little anxiety, but it's controlled—like that roller-coaster—and we ourselves remain perfectly safe. It's vicarious danger, and our brains love it.

Exercise: Begin with Danger
Write a scene that begins with danger. Start with an arresting line that signals a sense of danger right away ("It was a pleasure

to burn" worked all right for Ray Bradbury in *Fahrenheit 451*) and then proceed to depict a scene in which a character is in physical and/or emotional peril.

Note that it doesn't matter that the reader doesn't know who this character is. Our brains tune in to danger, not "danger but only if we know the person." Remember what you felt when I described the toddler and the tall grass with the cobra in it?

That fact helps you in your novel's opening scene, because most likely, the reader won't already be familiar with the character you feature.

Now take a look at some of your own stories and see which of them start with something that would catch a reader's attention with danger . . . and which don't.

Finally, it's not only the beginning of your novel that ought to begin with danger. Every time you begin a chapter or scene—and at multiple points *within* or at the end of scenes—you need to use something that re-engages the reader. Depicting risk or danger is a great way to keep her attention on your story.

Hacking the Reader's Attention Through Surprise

There's one more thing the human brain is constantly scanning for: the unexpected.

The brain is a comparison machine. From the moment we're born, our brains are taking in images, sensations, and other input for the first time. Babies are constantly receiving new data and new experiences, and their brains are collating it all, finding shelf space for it, and trying to analyze it all. No wonder babies sleep all the time!

But after awhile, they've stored enough experiences to form a base understanding of their world. From that point on, everything they encounter that fits with that base is either a pleasant thought—"Yes, that's Mommy again" or "Hey, there's my toy!"—or one that leaves the baby bored—"Yup, that's still the wall."

But everything that doesn't fit with that base of known experiences, everything new or surprising or unexpected, restarts the attentional circuits and makes Baby look on with wide eyes.

When we get older and cooler—[cough] teenagers [cough]— it takes a lot to surprise or impress us. We've seen it all and we are not amused.

That's okay, my dear Youth of +4 All-Knowing . . . I still know how to getcha.

Let's say a class full of teens (or adults) are slumping in their chairs while some boring, wrinkly, old dude (like, maybe 30 years old!) stands there droning on about some stupid subject, and then a trio of rhesus monkeys scampers into the room and begins swinging from the light fixtures.

I promise you that every person in that room, young or old, would stop paying attention to the speaker (or phone) and would immediately shift attention to the monkeys. They wouldn't even be able to not look.

The power of the surprising, the unexpected, the previously non-indexed, and the intriguing is wired in. I guarantee that if you present something fascinating to your reader, you will have her attention.

Surprise is irresistible. Try to not look or flinch when someone unexpectedly makes a loud sound near you. Just try it. When faced with the unexpected, your brain will force you to turn all its data-collecting sensors toward the anomaly and remain focused on it until it is categorized and assessed.

So it is with fiction. Surprise and intrigue your reader, and her attention will be yours.

Note that it's your *reader* you're trying to surprise here, not necessarily the character in the scene. Sometimes the character will be confused or intrigued by what happens too, but very often that's not the case. For example, if your character leaves his house, gets into his car, and *flies* away, the chances are good that the character won't be surprised by this. "Whoa! When did I get a flying car?" Yeah, probably not. But if you play it right, the reader will be surprised, and thus engaged.

When your reader's brain encounters something that doesn't fit the known pattern, Dr. Zak taught me, the "attentional circuits" cause her to try to gain more information. She pays attention, in other words.

Maybe your novel isn't the kind that would begin with the sort of physical or emotional danger I described earlier. If starting with action wouldn't be right for your book, you can still hack your reader's brain through something that doesn't fit the known pattern. Write a scene that is fascinating, intriguing, surprising, and otherwise arresting, and your reader's brain will be hacked for sure.

You could show a woman learning an intricate ballet sequence. Put us inside the mind and muscles of this dancer. Use sharp and sensual vocabulary to give granularity to the moment.

You could show a man taking exquisite care in laying out pieces of medieval armor and driving away gawkers and promising that everyone will understand once *she* arrives.

One caveat: Don't be so different and unexpected as to be baffling. I once read an unpublished novel in which a character was teaching in a classroom and then was suddenly in a new scene in a car and a person's body was catapulted across the top.

Well, yes, that was all very surprising. But I wasn't intrigued—I was disoriented. If I'd been able to keep my bearings better, I might've been engaged by the unexpected nature of it all. But I was jerked around and confused. It wasn't my attentional circuits that were engaged; it was my let's-go-find-something-we-can-actually-understand circuits.

Finally, *humor* is a form of surprise that works to engage the reader. One of my favorite openings for a novel is from Douglas Adams' *The Restaurant at the End of the Universe*: "In the beginning, the universe was created. This has made a lot of people very angry and been widely regarded as a bad move." Even if I didn't already know that this novel was hysterical, that first line would make me keep reading. It catches my attention through that unexpected and startling statement, which also happens to be fairly funny.

Exercise: Begin with Surprise
Write a scene that catches the reader's attention through the unexpected or the fascinating, the surprising or the funny.

Teach us something we know nothing about. Raise a mystery in our minds. Take us to a forbidden or fantastical place. Show us a character behaving in wildly unexpected ways. Thrust us inside a magical storm. Surprise us with an unusual twist, like having the sweet little girl pour milk in a saucer and cat food in a bowl and then put it down in front of the waiting . . . old man.

Both/And

Catching your reader's attention is your first and only job at the beginning of a novel. Some readers may give you only one page to catch their attention. Some readers, like me, will give you only one *line.*

If you don't indicate to my brain, in that first handful of words, that this is something I *must* pay attention to, I'll believe you. I'll move on to something else that does signal interest to my waiting neurons. So will most of your readers.

How many novels I see—even some that have been published—that begin with something exceedingly boring, mundane, usual, ordinary, and safe. Person waking up from a nap.

Student doodling on a paper. Child feeding ducks. You might as well tell the reader that there is nothing to see here and she should just move along.

Heed Dr. Zak's first video! Remember the father and son walking in the zoo! Remember the fMRI and blood draw and survey results. Give boring, get boring. Give the mundane and safe, get a bored reader who moves on to something that will make her neurons fire. Don't be boring!

The good news is that your reader's brain is a fruit ripe for the picking. She's wide open for a brain hack. She simply cannot ignore danger or surprise. If you put those things in front of her eyes, she *will* pay attention. If you don't, she probably won't, either. It's as easy, and as automatic, as that.

But let's double our guarantee. If capturing the reader's attention is the single most important thing we must do at the beginning of a novel, let's pull out all the stops, shall we? Let's get her with danger *and* surprise. Let's put a character in a dangerous *and* intriguing situation. Let's show her in a situation of emotional suspense and physical peril as she attempts some fascinating feat we've never imagined in an exotic location we've never been.

You must grab your reader's attention—not only at the outset but especially at the outset. Now you know how to do it. Now you are master of the powers of irresistibility. Use them on your reader. She will express her deep thanks to you . . . by reading what you've written next.

Exercise: Begin with Both Danger and Surprise
Write a scene—an opening scene or just any scene—that combines both peril and intrigue for your reader. Engage that poor reader's brain with two things she simply can't ignore.

This can work for a novel of any kind. If your book is a light comic romance, the danger could be the emotional or relationship danger of having a potential boyfriend catch the young woman in an embarrassing situation, and the surprise can be the hilarious things she does to avoid discovery.

If you're writing something in which actual danger could be present, I think you'll know what to do.

Bring the danger, bring the unexpected, and rest in the confidence that you have your reader's attention.

4

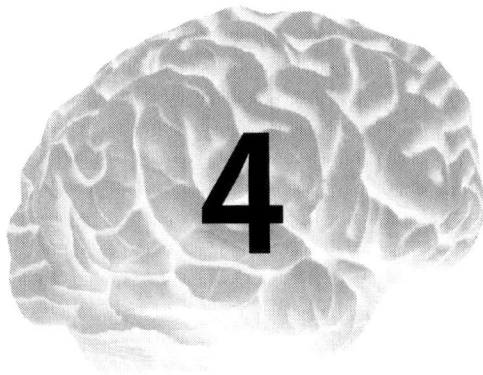

Connecting the Reader to Your Hero

Catching the reader's attention is your first task in engaging her from beginning to end. But that's just the beginning of the process.

Imagine a carnival barker calling out to people passing by. He first has to get someone to look at him, to stop and listen, before he can begin to give his spiel and hopefully make a sale. So the carny calls out, "Step right up, folks! Play the game and win a prize. Every player a winner. What about you, ma'am? Do you think the young man at your side has what it takes to toss a ring to win a prize? What about you, sir—fancy a dance with Lady Luck? Step right up, I say. Step right up!"

Once he's got people on the line, he can begin reeling them in. Getting them on the line isn't the sale, but it's a step he couldn't make the sale without.

So it is with your fiction. You're using brain science to catch the reader's attention, and you can't thrill the reader with your amazing story that is to come without piquing her interest. But doing so is just the prelude to the real action, which we'll talk about now.

The Key to It All

There is one secret ingredient to crafting a novel that readers will read from beginning to end. All the other elements are important and necessary, but in the end, they play supporting roles to this one.

The secret to engaging your reader from beginning to end is to connect her to your protagonist.

"I couldn't stop thinking about the characters, even when I wasn't reading the book."

"The heroine felt like my best friend. I wish I could meet her."

"I fell in love with Timothy and Jasmine."

"I had to find out if she ever reconciled with her father."

"It's weird, but I almost thought that whole crazy adventure was happening to *me*."

"It was amazing getting to go through those events in someone else's shoes."

"I felt like I was right there in the middle of it."

"I kept forgetting she wasn't real. I even caught myself praying for her once."

"If I ever got into a war, I'd like to think I'd be as heroic as he was."

These are all ways of saying one thing: "I was *there*. I was so connected to the character that the line was blurred between what was happening in the story and what was happening to me. It even became a little fuzzy whether I was observing this person's trauma or somehow participating in it. All I know is that I felt like I'd been through it, and I loved every minute!"

We're talking about a psychological phenomenon called *transportation*.

Transportation Excitation

I previously mentioned the human brain's ability to allow us to feel things vicariously, even if all we're doing is hearing someone else's story.

That's transportation, and it's why storytelling is a thing.

Imagine a group of cavemen sitting around the fire one evening, eating roast mammoth. Zog says, "You know, it was a night just like this, at just about this time, that my brother stood up from this very fire and walked into the jungle alone and unarmed. A saber-toothed tiger ate him."

The other people nod sagely and then, when they're done eating, stand up and walk into the jungle alone and in different directions.

You guessed it: Some of them weren't in attendance at the next night's fireside dinner.

That's what happens when transportation *doesn't* occur. When we're not able to get out of our own heads and place ourselves into someone else's, we fail to learn the lessons that could save our lives. We also fail to experience the joys of others and the sorrows of others. We miss the entire opportunity to grow through the experiences of others.

Happily, the Zog clan's lack of transportation ability has not survived to modern times. If you're reading this book, the odds are very good that you can indeed identify with what other people are going through. I'm willing to bet you can also feel what other people are feeling—even fictional people.

Which explains why you got misty-eyed at the end of that movie. Transportation explains why you squeezed your partner's arm off during that horror film. And it certainly explains why, when the hero was hanging from the cliff while the villain stomped on his fingers, your palms were sweating.

Why did *you* cry and squeeze and sweat? Why did you laugh and rejoice and fret? Why did you worry when the character got hurt and feel relieved when she was shown to be okay? You weren't actually in those situations. Except, you kind of were.

We get into our stories, don't we? We feel them utterly, whether it's a novel, a movie, a play, or a story someone relates. We have the ability to place ourselves in the skin of other people.

This is very, very good news for those of us who are storytellers.

The question, of course, is how to *cause* readers to make that jump into our characters' skin. We've all read stories that left us cold and did not get us to feel any kinship or concern for the characters. Worse, we may've even read stories in which we came to hope that misfortune would come to the characters.

We know it's possible for readers to feel deeply for fictional characters, and we know it's possible for readers to not give a rip for fictional characters. We want our readers to do the former, not the latter, because that's the secret to keeping them engaged from beginning to end—but we may not know how. How can we cause transportation to happen, and how can we be certain it *will* happen?

We hack the reader's brain, of course!

Emotional Engagement

How do we become friends with people?

Let's say you sit down next to a stranger on an airplane, and let's say you two end up talking during the flight. Might you become friends? Possibly. Perhaps you've had the experience, as I have, of falling into an excellent conversation in such a situation. Probably, when the flight ends, you simply give each other a merry goodbye and go your separate ways. But sometimes, you might have hit it off so well that you promise to stay in touch after the flight.

And in some rare cases, people meet on a flight as strangers and go on to became lifelong friends. Indeed, Dr. Zak met his future wife on an airplane.

How does something like this happen? Let's look at it, because it explains how readers come to care about fictional characters.

When strangers begin to talk, they may find they have things in common. Recently, I sat next to another dad at my daughter's elementary school as we waited for the kids to go to class. We were of different ethnicities and ages. But we'd seen each other on previous mornings and of course we both had children at the same school, so we already had some things in common.

This particular Monday morning in November, I asked him if he'd seen any of the pro football games over the weekend, and he said he had. I asked if he'd seen the Dallas Cowboys' game, and he had. It had been a fantastic game with a thrilling and wonderful finale (for Cowboys' fans, anyway!), and both of us got more animated as we talked and laughed about the game.

Our common experience of watching the game, along with our common enthusiasm for it, was a bridge we built across a number of significant differences that might otherwise have divided us. But the best was yet to come.

He shared a story about how, as a child, he'd had an experience with his dad's reaction to a Cowboys' game on TV that had caused him to have strong feelings about the team. That was astonishing, because I'd personally had a very similar experience as a child. I'd been only 4 and hadn't previously paid attention to sports, but one day my father and grandfather had started yelling at the TV for some reason. I started paying attention and learned that the Dallas Cowboys were trying to win a big game. I asked what the Dallas Cowboys were, and that started my lifelong love of the team and the sport.

Now, my new friend's strong feelings for the Cowboys were negative ones (lol), but the point was that we'd both had remarkably similar experiences as children about the same NFL team. It was a fantastically bonding moment, and I now look forward to talking with him in the mornings before school begins.

See how that worked? I found things in him that were similar to me, and suddenly I felt I knew him. Or I felt I could understand a little of what it might be like to be him, because in this one way at least, we were very similar. It made me think we would probably be friends in general.

I also found admirable qualities in him—that is to say, qualities I like in myself!—such as liking pro football, laughing about games, enjoying the struggle of sports, and trying to be humble when our teams win and gracious when they lose. I began to see myself in this person, and that made me like him.

Sounds narcissistic, I know, but you do it too.

We can use this phenomenon to cause our readers to like our characters: by causing them to see themselves in our characters. When we show characters who are like our readers, mainly in good and admirable ways, our readers will like them. They will begin to connect, to bond, to be transported.

Can you think of a way to show that your hero is friendly? Your reader will like him if you do. Can you show your hero being brave and standing up against injustice or bullies? Your reader will admire him if you do. Can you show your hero being generous or forgiving or responsible? What about scrupulously honest—returning a man's dropped wallet untouched even though your hero needs a dollar to eat—unashamedly loyal, or earnest and hard-working?

Show your hero as the kind of person your reader would like if she met, and transportation will begin. Show your hero as the kind of person your reader aspires to be like, and transportation will accelerate.

When you cause your reader to feel that your hero is like her, or is what she'd like to become, she will become emotionally engaged.

Now I'd like to bring in some help from a surprising and marble-carved source.

A Single Soul Dwelling in Two Bodies

The Greek philosopher Aristotle gave that "two bodies" quote as his definition of a friend. When it comes to fiction, we're shooting for that sort of relationship between the reader and the hero.

Our ancient friend studied many things in his historic career, but many people don't know he applied his mind to hacking people's brains.

His book *Rhetoric* reveals the findings of his studies in how to get people to feel what he wanted them to feel. In the context of a legal case, Aristotle wanted to give speakers the ability to cause judges and listeners to become predisposed to rule in the speakers' favor. He wanted to manipulate—er, persuade—people to like who he wanted them to like and dislike who he wanted them to dislike.

We're concerned with connecting our reader with our hero, and Aristotle has some strikingly effective methods for doing so.

Aristotle's secret is to demonstrate that the person in question (i.e., your hero) possesses qualities the listeners (your readers) admire or will resonate with.

His first approach is to show that the person is friendly or would be a good friend. If you can cause your reader to feel that this character is someone with whom she'd probably be friends, transportation has begun. You do this by showing the hero being friendly toward people or animals, being kind and generous. Standing up for the oppressed, being charming, behaving in nice and pleasant ways, and acting admirably. Sounds familiar, doesn't it?

Show the person being quick to forgive. Show him believing the best about others. Show him being kind toward someone we ourselves would wish kindness to come to. If you can manage it, show your hero being nice to someone who is probably very much like your reader. We like people who are nice to people like us. Show him being a loyal friend, an honest but loving counselor, and a person who makes the weak feel protected.

By contrast, I think of the Marquis Evremonde in Charles Dickens' *A Tale of Two Cities*. He races his carriage through Paris for the sport of seeing the peasants clear out of his way. He runs down a little boy, killing him, and tosses a few coins to Gaspard, the grieving father, to compensate him for his loss. Use this to your advantage too: Showing a character who is *not* nice or friendly or admirable is a great way of making the reader *dislike* him.

Aristotle hits upon the strongest one of all, compassion, but I'm going to save that one for the next section. I will say that if you show your hero *being* compassionate and showing sympathy, your reader will like him.

He recommends showing the person as being worthy of emulation. If you show the hero as someone we would admire or even revere in real life, your reader will connect with him. Even showing the hero doing the actual admiring is powerful, as when you might show him going out of his way to help a veteran. If you make your reader surge with pride and admiration for the hero, she will like him. She will become emotionally engaged.

Exercise: Show a Likable Character
Write a scene in which you show the hero being likable in some way. Maybe she's friendly or generous or compassionate. Maybe she stands up for a friend who is being maligned behind her back. Maybe she tells the truth even though it gets her in trouble.

You don't have to go too crazy and show nine saintly things the person does all in one Disney princess scene. Just pick an admirable attribute and write a scene that shows how that is a characteristic of this person.

Exercise: Show an Unlikable Character
Then have fun writing about a character you really don't want the reader to like. Show him being despicable or abusive or dishonest. Show him cheating an innocent out of a deserved reward. Show him throwing someone else under the bus, literally or figuratively, to save his own sorry skin.

It can be delicious fun to write bad guys. Note that such a scene may have the dual and opposite effect of making us care about the other guy, the person this villain has done wrong. That's because we feel sad for people who are hurting.

Which makes for a terrific segue into the next section.

It's a Rock—It Doesn't Have Any Vulnerable Spots!

Tim Allen's character in *Galaxy Quest* had trouble getting away from an alien rock monster, despite his crewmate's "helpful" advice to attack its vulnerable spots.

While rocks don't *have* any vulnerable spots, your protagonist does. And when you reveal these vulnerabilities in the story, your reader will not be physically capable of disliking him.

If you think that sounds like brain hacking language, you're right.

When you feel compassion toward someone—when you feel *empathy*—there is an automatic reaction in your brain. Oxytocin, the neurotransmitter I mentioned earlier, gushes into your brain. It is received by the many oxytocin receptors in your brain, causing you to feel a strong bond with the person and a powerful impulse to get up and take action to relieve the person's distress.

When you see a toddler get knocked over and begin to cry, the chances are good that you're going to wish you could rush forward and pick the baby up. That's oxytocin doing a number on your brain.

(As an aside, if you're wondering why I almost always refer to your reader as a female, oxytocin is the explanation. Women's brains release more oxytocin than men's brains do for the same stimuli. When a man sees a toddler get knocked over, he feels empathy. When a woman sees a toddler get knocked over, she feels empathy-times-two (at least). This ability to feel for others, to connect with others through empathy, explains why women constitute 80% of the entire readership of fiction. They find it easy and fun to connect with people in fiction, as in life. Women readers of fiction outnumber male readers, even for Westerns and military fiction. It will behoove you to begin thinking of your reader as female, because that's most likely the case.)

When you see a puppy being terrorized by a bigger dog (or by a human), don't you want to just stride in and come to the rescue? Those terrified eyes! That cringing posture! Even if you manage not to leap up from your seat, inside, your brain *is* leaping up.

When you see a nerdy young man standing on the girl's doorstep with a bouquet of flowers behind his back, and then the clichéd jock comes up, pushes him aside, strides in, takes the pretty girl in his arms, and lays a big kiss on her, you feel for the first boy, don't you? You want to give that arrogant jock a piece of your mind—or your fist.

When we witness someone in pain, in fear, in need—when we see someone *vulnerable*—we can't help but want to rise up and do something. And if we're not there in person but are only *reading* about the situation in which someone is being victimized and whose vulnerabilities are being exposed and exploited, we obviously know we can't do anything to help that person ourselves. So what we do instead is scoop up a ginormous helping of compassion and place it on that person in our minds. Every time we read about that person from there on out, we see him through the lens of empathy.

In other words, we're pulling for him.

We place the force of our good wishes beneath his name.

We adopt him into our hearts. Now he's not just some random person on the page; now he's *our guy.*

And when our guy faces his next challenge, we're right there with him. We're in his corner. We pull for him to win. We'd be willing to rough up a whole legion of bad guys to give our guy his chance.

That, my friend, is transportation.

Wherever our guy goes for the rest of the story, we're not only behind him, we have in some sense *become* him. We've identified with his cause and his pain so completely that his pain is our pain, his loss is our loss, and his victory is, at last, our victory.

All through a little trick called vulnerability.

Show your hero hurting and vulnerable—not because he's a loser or a whiner-baby, but because he does right and yet is left in pain—and your reader will connect. She literally (and I do mean *literally*) cannot help herself.

Exercise: Make the Oxytocin Flow

Write a scene in which an innocent is harmed. That's the most basic way to say it. Show someone who isn't doing anything wrong and yet becomes the victim of some negative act, some injustice, or something that wounds him. Or you could show someone wanting to be noticed and liked and is feeling vulnerable, and yet that person doesn't receive the hoped-for response but rather something that leaves him feeling devastated.

I'm guessing you know what makes you feel empathy for someone. When I teach this material to teen writers (most of whom are female) and I tell that story about the little boy dying of cancer and his father hiding his grief to give the boy a last fun day at the zoo, an audible "Awww!" sweeps the auditorium. That's the sound of oxytocin, the sound of empathy.

What makes *you* say, "Awww"?

Write a scene that would do that to you, and you can know without doubt that your reader will instantly engage with that hurting character.

Vice and Glue

Your first job in a novel, as we've seen, is to catch your reader's attention. But really, that's just the carnival barker making you stop and not pass by. The real objective is to get your reader to come inside and become a customer. With fiction, the real goal at the outset of your novel is to forge a bond between your reader and your protagonist.

You catch the reader's attention through danger or surprise, and you connect the reader and hero by making her see that they're similar, by showing that the hero is likable, and by showing the hero's pain. What will carry your reader through to the end of your novel is engagement with the hero.

I like to think of this two-step process as someone gluing two pieces of wood together. There's a period when the glue hasn't set and won't hold the pieces the way you want. So you have to hold the pieces in place until the glue hardens and sets.

The ideal solution is to use one or more vice grips. These are squeeze- or twist-tightened clamps that hold things in position. So the glue goes on, the pieces go together, the vice grips get attached . . . and then you wait.

The thing to notice is that the technique holding the pieces together at first is not the technique that will hold the pieces together permanently. But the long-term fixative takes awhile to take effect, so you use a short-term solution until it does.

So it is with fiction. Your long-term solution to connecting your reader to your protagonist is the "glue" of empathy. You'll be using multiple moments and situations and approaches to create that tight bond that will last until the end of the novel and beyond. But those things take awhile to develop, so you need something to hold the reader to the story while they can. You need something keeping her reading until the empathy glue can set. That's what the attention-grabbing material is doing.

Engage her attention with danger and surprise. Engage her emotions, the longer fix, by connecting her to your hero.

Exercise: Your Vice and Glue
What could you use in your novel to catch your reader's attention? And then what could you do, while that temporary bond is holding, to begin showing how likable, admirable, and vulnerable your hero is?

By the way, there's nothing that says you can't be doing both of these at the same time. Catch her attention with something dangerous that shows your hero being treated unjustly, maybe. Show her doing something fascinating while comforting a frightened child.

Also, you'll be doing these things throughout your novel, not just at the beginning. You certainly need to catch your reader's attention at the outset, but you will need to re-catch her attention again and again over the course of the story. And at the beginning you certainly need to connect your reader to the hero, but you'll need to continue deepening that bond the whole time.

There's never a bad time to re-engage your reader's attentional circuits, and it's always the right time to show something likable, admirable, or oxytocin-generating about your hero.

I can't emphasize enough the importance of these two techniques. Do them, and you'll hack your reader's brain. Don't do them, and you won't. Everything else depends on the vice and the glue.

5

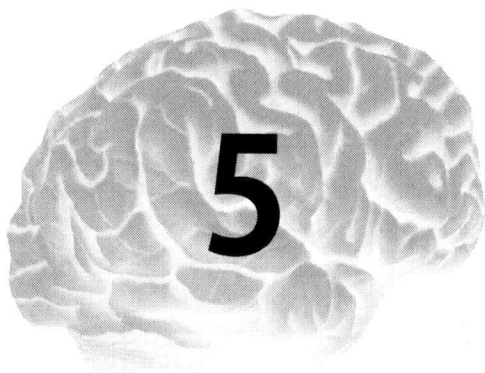

Conjuring Dragons

There's one more thing you must do at the beginning of your novel in order to secure your reader's total engagement: You must give your hero a massive challenge.

Your hero is only as valiant as the obstacle he faces. If the armored knight rides out and, by feat of arms, vanquishes a . . . mouse . . . that's not going to make him seem very heroic.

What's worse, if the challenge you set before your hero is that easily overcome, you will fail to engage your reader. Nobody wants to watch David face off against Tiny Tim. But we all want to see David fight Goliath.

Indeed, if David fights Tiny Tim, he's the *villain* in that story, not the hero. But throw an avalanche at him, and he's not only the hero, he's the underdog, and now we can't not watch.

To hack your reader's brain, you must conjure dragons. That same knight, faced with a fire-breathing monstrosity that just demolished the strongest castle in the realm, becomes "our guy" in this struggle, and we'll watch very, very carefully to see what happens. Especially if you've done your job of bonding us to this knight so we not only pull for him but also feel as if we *are* him. We won't be able to stop reading.

Let's say you've done a great job catching my attention with a fabulous beginning (what Dr. Zak calls "a hot open") and have deeply endeared this hero to me, and then you show that the struggle this amazing hero is going to face is . . . installing a pencil sharpener.

You're going to lose me quick. Maybe not instantly, because you've done so well at the outset, so I'll give you a few pages to get going. But if you don't show me right away that the pencil sharpener isn't really what his biggest challenge is going to be in this book, I'm leaving.

And what's more, I'll be ticked at you for making me care and making me believe this was going to be something special. Dr. Zak calls it brain confusion, and it's uncomfortable, to say the least.

Your reader is ready to believe that you know how to hook her up with the brain drugs she's jonesing for. Part of that involves an extremely difficult challenge set before your hero.

The Brain's Favorite Story

Our brains crave stories about *conflict*. Really, without struggle and resistance, you don't have drama at all—you have something that is routine, mundane, safe, and therefore boring. And we know what "boring" does to brain activity . . . and to reader engagement. (Don't be boring!)

The brain's favorite story is the story of struggle. Conflict, opposition, a challenge, a villain—these are the things your brain loves. In fiction, at least!

If you want to keep your reader engaged, there must be conflict. That's not to say you must have unrelenting conflict with no moments of respite (more on that in the next chapter).

But if you find your reader's mind wandering in a certain section, that's a prime place to insert conflict.

Whenever I teach this, I can't resist including a Harry Flugleman quote from *The Three Amigos*:

"All the great *Amigo* pictures had one thing in common: Three wealthy Spanish landowners who fight for the rights of peasants. Now, that's something everyone likes. It's a people idea. It's a story a nation can sink its teeth into. But then came *Those Darn Amigos*. A box office failure. Nobody went to see it. Because nobody cares about three wealthy Spanish landowners on a weekend in Manhattan. We strayed from the formula, and we paid the price."

You see the problem with *Those Darn Amigos*, don't you? No conflict. No dragons. Don't stray from the formula. Don't pay the price.

Exercise: Conjure a Dragon

What's an incredibly challenging struggle you could give a character? Think of a character from one of your stories; if you had to put her in her own story or in some new story, what challenge could you give her that would be perfect for her—perfectly impossible?

Now think of three levels of increase you could give to that challenge. If the conflict is to face a dragon, now say that it's a dragon that can disappear at will, a dragon that can also heal itself nearly instantly from any wound, and a dragon that can also become invulnerable at will. How's the hero going to defeat it now? The higher the difficulty of the challenge set before the hero, the higher your reader engagement will be.

Engagement Formula

Speaking of not straying from the formula, here's the brain hacking formula for securing reader engagement at the beginning of your novel:

Catch the attention + cause reader transportation + add massive conflict = reader engagement

All three elements are crucial. Happily, all three are automatically accomplished simply by taking what we know of how the brain works and using it to our advantage.

The movie *Whiplash* is a great example of all three elements working in concert.

The story begins with a scene in which a young man is alone at night in a darkened school playing drums. He's doing so in a way that shows he's adept at the instrument. (That's intriguing to me because I don't know anything about jazz drumming, so it engages with surprise/fascination.)

Into the practice room comes an older man who the drummer obviously knows and is obviously intimidated by. The man tells him gruffly to play a certain style, and the drummer begins to do so. (That's further intriguing, because I'm learning more about this new realm of music.) The drummer has only barely begun when the old man cuts him off as if disgusted. (Now my sympathy for the drummer is beginning to grow, because that wasn't a nice way to treat this kid, who is obviously trying hard.)

Time after time, the old man gives the drummer a command on how to play, and time after time, the drummer shows he's up to the challenge. (So my admiration for him in the face of adversity is growing.) But every time, the old man cuts him off, as if growing more and more disapproving, and the young man grows more and more desperate. (That has the dual effect of increasing my connection with the drummer and increasing my dislike for this curmudgeon. Note also that my attention is further engaged by the element of emotional danger the drummer is now feeling. He seems to feel that something very important is at risk here, and that makes me lean forward in attention and concern.)

The old man gives the drummer a final instruction, and the drummer begins. He's sweating now, but his play sounds flawless to me. This time, the old man doesn't interrupt his playing, so we're beginning to feel slightly hopeful for him. He pushes himself so hard, to the point that drops of sweat and blood are falling on the drums. He plays and plays and brings the set to a fantastic finish, and he looks up, panting heavily.

The old man is gone.

We suspect he's been gone the entire time, the old jerk.

I remember my compassion all but erupting in that moment. This kid just played his heart out for this disapproving ogre and he doesn't even have the decency to tell him he's leaving? Oh, this poor kid. At that moment, I felt like I could come to fisticuffs on behalf of . . .

A fictional character.

Oh, right. I sort of forgot this wasn't real.

Look at how the filmmakers hacked my brain. They caught my attention with surprise (fascination/intrigue) and then emotional danger (i.e., they used *both* ways of catching attention). They showed me a story that would have massive conflict—not only in the world of competitive jazz but also in opposition to that old man as villain. And then, at the same time (in the same *scene*) as all that, they also made me feel so incredibly compassionate toward this young drummer. I remember feeling that I didn't care *what* this young man was going to go through, I was going to go through it with him. I was hooked.

Rather, I was hacked.

And I loved it.

(*Whiplash* is a brutal movie to watch, by the way. Do so at your own peril. But I suspect, after the opening scene, you may find it difficult not to stick it out to the end.)

As powerful as that scene was, there's nothing at all mysterious about why it worked. They followed the brain hacking formula, and humans simply can't resist.

I don't know about you, but I'm tired of feeling around in the dark in my fiction and just hoping my stories will be engaging. It's so relieving to have tools that work so I can know my reader is right where I want her.

Which means that if you follow the brain hacking formula too, the humans who read your book won't be able to resist either.

6

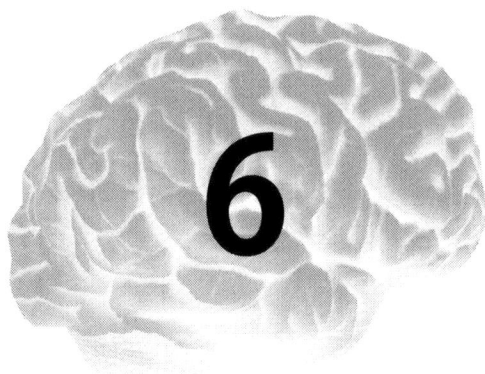

Increasing Reader Engagement Through Act 2

Many novelists do a pretty good job of starting their books, and they can craft a strong climax and conclusion. But where they lose reader engagement is in Act 2. The dreaded sagging middle.

If you've got a big story, you've got a vast expanse between the hot open and the crackerjack finish. Over the centuries, novelists have tried many gimmicks for keeping the middle of a book interesting. Some authors, when they sense the momentum lagging, just kill a character. Others look for a plot twist or reversal. Still others try to prop up that drooping roof with flashbacks or subplots.

Dr. Zak calls it "nearly miraculous" to cause a reader to keep turning pages. "Boredom creeps in easily," he says, because "the brain wants the 'new, new thing.' If a story seems predictable and safe, we lose interest."

Perhaps you've encountered a book or movie in which the primary conflict is resolved too early. As soon as that happens, the suspense (and, with it, reader/viewer engagement) drops through the floor. If our hero is completely safe and the bad guy is dealt with, why aren't the credits rolling? Why is there still so much book left?

We see this in series on TV. As soon as the primary male and the primary female stop ignoring the romantic tension between them and become a couple, ratings drop. Why? Because the thing that was at risk (the will-they-or-won't-they question) has been dealt with, and we instantly lose interest. The suspense is gone. Many shows that allow those two to be a couple will be cancelled soon after.

Some shows try to mitigate this safe/boring loss in ratings by coming up with artificial ways to keep the couple apart—delaying the wedding, breaking them up, having one partner abducted for months, etc. (*Castle*, I'm lookin' at you)—in a failed attempt to keep viewer engagement. Shows may fail for other reasons than just that, but it is true that, when you solve one of the big areas of conflict and tension in a story, viewers and readers are ready for your book to be done.

Tension, it seems, is a huge element in reader engagement.

Act 2 Awesomeness

In a sense, I get confused when authors say Act 2 is where the tension falls off.

Maybe it's because I think about three-act structure out of order. In my mind, Act 2 is the delicious creamy center of a story, it's the actual fun you wanted to have in this book, the reason (plot-wise) you thought this would be a good story in the first place. I don't think of Act 2 as this vast wasteland between the great opening and the great conclusion. I personally think of it as almost more fun *than* the opening and the conclusion.

Act 2 is where Indiana Jones goes after the lost Ark, for crying out loud. Act 2 is where Luke Skywalker rescues a princess, comes of age, and escapes the Death Star. Act 2 is where

Scrooge meets all the ghosts. Act 2 is where the crew of the *Nostromo* tries to kill a bloodthirsty alien and where Quint, Brody, and Hooper go after the killer shark and realize they're going to need a bigger boat. Act 2 is where Phil Connors tries to escape his recurring Groundhog Day and the Ghostbusters go after the ghosts. Act 2 is where Rick and Ilsa rekindle their love and try to escape Casablanca before they're rounded up with the usual suspects.

Act 2 is the fun! How could it ever be boring if it's the centerpiece and *raison d'être* for the story in the first place?

Here's what I mean by how I think of three-act structure out of order. I start by establishing the awesomeness I want to do in Act 2, and I go from there.

Let's pull from the previous chapter and say that I want to write a story about a young knight who decides he must slay the mammoth dragon terrorizing his homeland. The Act 2 of that story is going to be just that, his multiple attempts to find and kill the dragon. It will involve new allies and foes, new setbacks and breakthroughs, and much character growth. But that hunt or duel between those two forces is the fun I want to have with this book, so that's Act 2. Not boring or saggy at all.

Act 1, then, is simply all the stuff I need to do so I can get to Act 2. Simple, right? Before I can have that duel, I need to establish our hero as he is when the story begins. I need to establish that the dragon is out there and is a terrible, man-eating menace. I need to establish our hero's reason for wanting to go after said dragon—the stakes. I need to establish who his primary relationships are, what his "normal" is like, and what's exceptional about him. I need to be connecting the reader to him and all the other brain science stuff. Finally, he needs to decide to do it and to take his first strides toward his fiery destiny.

As soon as I've set all that up, I can start doing the man vs. dragon story that is Act 2.

But that hunt can't go on forever. Eventually, I need to end the story and bring things to a conclusion. That's all Act 3 is: bringing things to a head and then tying them off. So eventually, after many adventures and much inner journeying, our hero finally has the dragon cornered and can mount his last desperate assault on the beast. He attacks, he wins or loses, and then we show how the realm is after the dust settles.

The beginning of that novel would be amazing and the climax would be tremendous, but I don't see a single boring, saggy thing in the middle.

Hack your own brain by changing how you think of Act 2, and you may find reader engagement staying strong all through that thrilling middle.

The Brain Hacker's Tools

Brain science has given us two major tools for hacking reader engagement through the middle of your novel: the sine wave and anticipation.

But before I look at those, I want to remind you that you can and should use, throughout your novel, the neuroscience tools I've already given you. Do we need to catch the reader's attention at the beginning of the novel only? No, we need to do so throughout. It's always a good time to use the brain hacking tools of danger and the unexpected. Do we need to cause the reader to feel empathy for our hero at the beginning only? No, we need to do so all along the way. Keep playing that likability and vulnerability card in a variety of ways. Is the beginning the only place where it's appropriate to show that the hero is up against a huge challenge or foe? You guessed it.

Don't think of these as specialty tools you'll use only once or twice at specific spots in your novel and then leave behind. Think of them as a growing accumulation of paintbrushes laid out beside your easel for quick access whenever the mood strikes you to use them in your painting in progress.

The Sine Wave

I said in the previous chapter that one of the ways to hack your reader's brain is to use tension and conflict—our conjured dragons. It would make sense that a slow and unrelenting increase of tension across the entire manuscript would be a great way to keep the reader engaged.

Unfortunately, that doesn't work. The brain gets tired.

"You can't keep the pedal to the metal all the time," Dr. Zak says. "The brain can't stay in fight-or-flight mode endlessly, or it will begin having undesirable side effects."

If only brain science could come to our rescue again . . .

Wish granted!

A sine wave, as you may or may not remember from your math classes of yesteryear, is a nice wavy line. It has equal ups and downs. It's most tranquil to look at.

When it comes to hacking your reader's brain, think of your Act 2 as a sine wave with the ups representing heightened tension and the downs representing little breathers or breaks.

Even in the midst of a titanic Act 2 about men hunting a killer great white shark, the characters had time for storytelling, reminiscing, and even a bit of laughter. Uninterrupted tension will tire out the reader's brain.

There's a reason Shakespeare's tragedies had silly nurses and rhyming rogues. Those breaks give the ol' noodle a breather, allowing it to go back and take even more tragedy. Comic relief, it turns out, is brain hacking.

It works the other way too, incidentally. If you're writing a comedy, your reader's brain needs a break from the unrelenting hysterics. Go serious for a minute here and there in your book, and you'll be golden.

When tension rises on the sine wave, other neurotransmitters go to work in your reader's brain. Adrenaline spikes at the conflict and testosterone (yes, even in women) elevates when the hero doubles down and decides to face the challenge. When you give your reader a break from the seriousness and have some levity or let the man and woman finally go on a good date, your reader's brain will pump out dopamine and endorphins and she will love her life . . . and your book.

Exercise: Just Sine Here
Think of a storyline you have written, are writing, or want to write. Determine whether the story is primarily serious, funny, suspenseful, scary, or whatever else. Now brainstorm ten scenes, moments, characters, situations, and/or subplots you could bring in that would offer the perfect counterpoint to that primary mood.

If you're writing an action thriller, come up with ten scenes or elements that can be funny or light or romantic. If you're writing a gentle romance, think of ten bits of action you can put in there somewhere.

Anticipation

Have you ever found yourself still reading a book despite the fact that you'd pretty much lost interest in it because you just had to find out if the boy and girl ever got together? Or if they managed to save the kids on the bus? Or if the dog ever finds its way home?

That feeling that you couldn't rest until you'd at least gotten a question resolved is a sign that your brain had been hacked. Not fully, since you'd lost interest in the rest of the book. But it is yet another way to tap into brain chemistry to engage your reader. Anticipation is a biggie, and if you couple anticipation with all the other tools I'm giving you in this book, your reader will be engaged from beginning to end.

Gambling addicts, neuroscientists have found, are more about the pursuit of winning than the winning itself. What drives them is that heady hope, that intoxicating thrill, of the risk and *anticipation* that may or may not receive a payoff in the form of a payout. It's that moment just before the revelation that is sweetest, not the revelation itself.

What does that mean for novelists? It means we have to give clues and tantalizing hints about the mysteries in our story. It means we err on the side of incomplete crumbs, not all-you-can-eat buffets. It means we have to tease the reader with the promise of big revelations to come . . . but not until X happens. It means we have to reveal bits of the mystery, preferably in ways that make the reader's mind go down an unexpected and exciting new path.

The brain, Dr. Zak says, has an "inescapable need to know what is going to happen next. That's what keeps us awake at night reading. Our curiosity is aroused and our survival instincts kick in. It's a rush—literally: a dopamine rush." The brain loves finding clues that lead to anticipation of impending discovery.

Exercise: And in Walked . . .
Think about your current story and brainstorm ten new ways to create anticipation for your reader. Pose a riddle. Separate the answer to a plot or relationship question by one or more intervening scenes. Leave a scene at a cliffhanger and switch over to another storyline or two before coming back to resolve the tension.

Use this brain hack in ways large and small. Small can be the slight mystery of who is making sounds downstairs in the middle of the night. Large can be the revelation of the traitor or the real culprit behind the crime that launched the story. Murder mysteries have anticipation built in . . . which may explain their massive popularity in book, stage, and screen.

The Ticking Time Bomb

A great way to hack your reader's brain with anticipation is to use a ticking time bomb.

In fiction, a ticking time bomb is a portent about any critical event that will hit your story in the future. It could be an actual time bomb ticking down or it could be the imminent eruption of a volcano or that moment when the cracks in the dam finally enlarge enough to unleash devastation on the unsuspecting people below. It could be a countdown, like the looming end of a game or the fast-approaching date of the Christmas dance.

Put a ticking time bomb in your story, and it will generate anticipation from the moment you let the reader know about it.

The great thing about this tool is that it works even when you're not talking about it on the page. If an asteroid is hurtling toward Earth on a collision course, even when the humans planning to deflect it are having a romantic or comic moment, *the reader still feels* the approach of the asteroid. "Yes, yes: kiss, kiss, smooch, smooch. Get on with it already and hurry up and get out there and stop that rock from destroying us all!"

The movie *Titanic* has perhaps the best ticking time bomb I've ever seen. Everyone in the audience knows there is an iceberg in that ship's future. It's almost more delicious that the characters don't know about it. It amps the viewer up and further hacks her engagement—and there's not a thing she can do to resist it. Even in those scenes when they're not looking at the water, the viewer is feeling this slow constriction of her stomach because she knows doom is approaching.

Do *that* to your reader, and anticipation will hack her brain.

Exercise: She Da Bomb

Think of large, novel-length ticking time bombs (volcanos, plagues, tsunamis) and small ticking time bombs (she's leaving town tomorrow and still doesn't know how he feels; someone is in the house and he still doesn't know it; the baby's car seat isn't buckled) for your fiction.

Really mess with your reader's OCD, in other words. (Kidding!)

Brainstorm ten of these for your book and implement at least one of them today.

When you view Act 2 as the apex of fun and wonderfulness of your story, and when you employ anticipation and occasional breaks from your story's primary mood, plus maybe a big ol' time bomb a-ticking away, you won't have to worry about your reader losing interest in the mighty middle of your book.

7

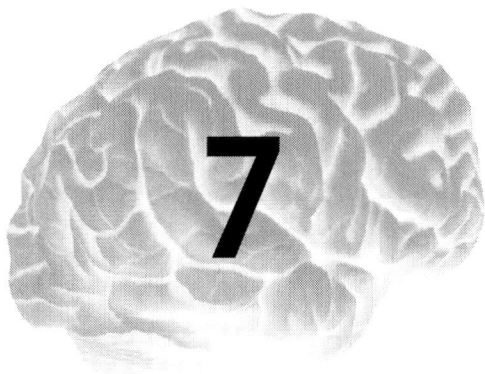

Fulfilling Reader Engagement in Act 3

By the time you get to Act 3, you almost won't have to worry about keeping your reader engaged.

If you've done what I recommend in this book, she will be hooked because she cares deeply about your hero and has to see her safely through to the end. She will be invested in seeing if her guesses about your plot will come out as she thinks. She will be full of curiosity and anticipation to see how the story resolves. She will be almost breathless because the time left on the bomb's countdown clock will be close to zero. She will be engaged because the biggest challenge of all is now before the hero's feet. She will be fascinated because what's going to happen is certainly new and previously uncategorized. And she will be enthralled because the highest danger or risk of the story is set to unfold.

She will, in short, be well and truly brain-hacked at this point.

There are, however, three essential hacks left to make. Here, as you send your story to its climax and then tie everything off, we're not so much talking about increasing reader engagement as we are about *fulfilling* reader engagement by making sure we give the reader's brain what it wants at the conclusion of any story.

Hero Transformation

Most of us haven't tried to articulate what exactly we're looking for when we come to fiction we read, but brain science tells us that one thing we're looking for is a hero who makes a change. An inner change. Character growth.

We want to see an epiphany. The hero's struggle, of course, is our struggle. We've fought alongside him on every page, exulting in his wins and feeling the pain and soul-searching of his losses. He is navigating something of life's difficulties, and we—vicarious learners, all—have assigned him as our guide through those difficulties too.

When he has his moment of truth, when he makes his key realization, we have it right there with him. Our brains release *glutamate,* the neurotransmitter involved in learning, and we feel a sense of calm and certainty, caused by *GABA* (Gamma-aminobutyric acid).

We want to see him look deep inside himself and attain enlightenment that transforms him. And then we want to see him use his newfound wisdom as he strides forward to face the final confrontation.

Exercise: Transformations
Brainstorm five epiphanies or realizations a hero might have at the climax of his or her inner journey. Then write out how he or she would employ that new consciousness in an external confrontation with the villain or the crucial moment in a plot that could go with it.

Resolution of the Plot Problem

The second thing your reader needs to have happen as your story hits its high point is that the main challenge of the plot needs to be dealt with.

If a big shark has been eating the people of your town, the book needs to end either with the shark dead or all the people dead or gone. You have to tie it off. If your story is a big will-they-or-won't-they romance in which two characters might or might not get together romantically, then you'd jolly well better allow or permanently prevent their union. Don't leave us hanging.

"We have tested narratives in which the climax does not resolve the dilemma," Dr. Zak says, "and there is a sort of brain confusion, because the pattern is broken. This results in reader disengagement. The climax is the tension reliever. It should feel satisfying."

I pity those poor experiment volunteers whose lot it was to hear the unresolved stories. It reminds me of Sheldon Cooper in *Big Bang Theory*, who is driven crazy by unfinished sequences, like if someone were to say, "With liberty and justice for . . ." and then stop. It would almost make his brain be the thing that gives a big bang.

Your reader is like that. If your story is about X, make sure you fully conclude the story of X in your book.

Now, can you do trilogies or series and therefore not conclude everything in book 1? Of course. But please give your reader's brain what it needs to ease its frustration. Bring a major part of the story to a conclusion or at least a true stopping place. If it's a war epic that will be told over the course of three books, then at the end of book 1, at least fully end the first battle. The reader will be ready for a new beginning, or a new continuation, in book 2. But she's earned the relief—the GABA and the *serotonin* (the neurotransmitter that makes us feel happy and whole)—that comes at the end of a job well done.

Exercise: Did You Finish?
Think back over novels written by you or others. Identify the main plot problem each book dealt with and then write down how that plot problem was resolved . . . or wasn't resolved.

If you find you have not fully resolved the big plot problem in your book, or at least brought the story to a satisfying mini-resolution, consider how you could change it to do so.

When I ran my publishing house, I occasionally worked with authors whose stories were way too long for a single book. We decided to break these into book-length chunks. We might end up with a trilogy or a two-book couplet, but they weren't true series books with each one designed to stand alone. We were just stopping the story and chopping it apart. So we looked for natural breathers in the larger story, down times following major plot and/or character developments.

Do that for your stories too. You want to keep your reader engaged right on through to the end, and *at* the end, the reader's brain doesn't need new engagement so much as closure.

A Happy Ending

The final thing your reader's brain needs from your story is a good outcome for the hero.

I'm sorry to tell you, if what you really wanted to do was cause the hero to reject hope and kill himself, that your reader will be ticked at you if you do so. It's almost painful to the brain when that happens in a story we read or watch. Which is probably why there are so few movies with depressing endings. We want to feel good and hopeful at the end of a story.

You can do that with books sometimes, especially if you're self-publishing and don't mind low sales. But we've been talking about making a bestseller here, and I'd be willing to bet that over 95% of bestselling novels do have a happy ending.

Why is that? Why do we want a good outcome for the hero? Go back to chapter 4, "Connecting the Reader to the Hero." If we've connected so intimately with the hero that his danger makes *our* palms sweat, then we are deeply invested with this person, almost to the point where we see him as us. And unless we don't like ourselves, we want a great outcome for ourselves . . . and anyone we identify with and pull for and care about. Namely, your hero.

Now, we could make a distinction between a true happy ending and a happy outcome for the hero. King Theoden dies in *Return of the King,* which is not a happy ending, but it's still a good outcome for him because he feels absolved and at peace. You could have a sad or tragic ending, plot-wise, and still manage a happy outcome for the hero, I suppose.

But why do that sort of gymnastics? Your reader wants a happy ending. She wants that GABA and serotonin. I would argue that she's earned her little brain juice party for staying with you from beginning to end, so I recommend you give her one.

Exercise: A Happy Outcome

Think about your favorite stories, books or movies, and categorize them into those that have happy endings and those that do not. I'm guessing there are more of the former than the latter. Imagine a happy ending for each of the tragedies you picked, and imagine a tragic ending for each of the happy endings you picked. I wonder how your list would change with those new endings.

Now look at one of your own works of fiction and imagine it with both a bad outcome for your hero and also a good outcome.

Then tear up all the ideas for bad outcomes and give your reader's brain what it wants!

Run the Bases

The last part of the Great Commandment of Fiction is that you must keep your reader engaged through to the end. You do that by employing the brain hacking tools you've been using all along. But as you round the base toward home, make sure you finish by giving the reader's brain what it needs in order to complete the neurochemistry journey and feel that this has been a most amazing story that delivered from start to finish.

So she'll run out and tell all her friends they *have* to read it.

Conclusion

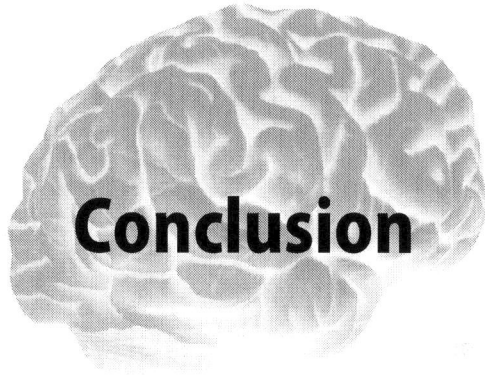

Your readers want their brains hacked. They're brain chemistry junkies hoping you have what they're needing to give them a story high. They're moviegoers deeply hoping you will make them feel that the time and money spent to be in this theater was well spent.

Fiction readers are looking for an experience. They expect to be engaged right away and not bored. Their brains expect, though they themselves might not be able to articulate it, to see conflict and tension that increase steadily over the course of the novel (though not without respite). They desperately want to find in your story a hero they can care about and cheer for and identify with. They want to see a person faced with incredible obstacles who somehow finds the courage to defeat it, and they want to see that hero learn something about himself along the way. Then, when the hero has had his epiphany, they want to see the big issue, the thing the story was about, well and truly resolved. Whew! He did it! And what's more, his life is meaningfully *improved* because of the events of this book.

If you don't give them these things—indeed, if you fail to give them *any* of these things—their engagement will lag and may lapse entirely. Don't be boring!

If you do use these tools, this is what they'll be saying about *your* book:

"I couldn't put it down!"

"I consumed it in one day and night—I think I forgot to eat."

"This should totally be a movie."

"I swear, I'm so excited about this book!"

"I wish these characters were my real friends. I feel like they are."

"I finished it and immediately started over from the beginning."

"You've *got* to read this book—I couldn't put it down."

Our hope for creating a bestseller rests with our ability to engage our reader from beginning to end.

And now you know how to do exactly that.

Acknowledgments

As I made clear throughout the book, I owe all the neuroscience information in this book to the work and instruction of Dr. Paul J. Zak.

Dr. Zak founding director of the Center for Neuroeconomics Studies and Professor of Economics, Psychology and Management at Claremont Graduate University. Dr. Zak also serves as Professor of Neurology at Loma Linda University Medical Center. He is the author of *The Moral Molecule,* and you can learn more about him at www.pauljzak.com.

I would also like to thank my beta readers, Patty Slack, Robi Ley, and Katie Hart, for their terrific comments and error correction, and my several endorsers for their amazing words.

Learn More

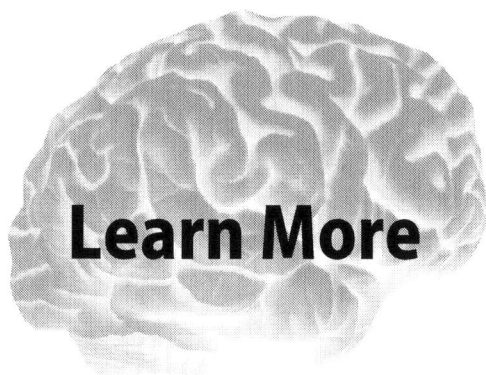

This material was first presented in Jeff's Writer's Digest book entitled *The Irresistible Novel.* There, it is part of a larger examination of the so-called "rules" of fiction (Part 1), the brain science of reader engagement (Part 2), and classical approaches to reader engagement (Part 3; Aristotle, Carl Jung, and Joseph Campbell).

If you enjoy Jeff's teaching in this e-book, you'll love him teaching on video. Jeff's online course, "Write Your Best Fiction and Get It Published" contains nearly 8 hours of in-studio video of Jeff teaching how to write great fiction. The course also includes Jeff's two interactive e-books, *How To Find Your Story* and *Character Creation for the Plot-First Novelist;* CharPick, his instant minor character generator; his white paper "The Horrific but True Psychological Phases of Writing a Novel," and more. The course runs for $200.

However, because you're a reader of this e-book, Jeff is offering you a discount of 75% off that price. For $49, an entire writers' conference-worth of world-class training is yours.

To get the discount, go to Udemy.com, search for Jeff's name or "Write Your Best Fiction and Get It Published," and enter the code BRAINHACK49.

Jeff would love to hear from you. Check out his writing, his freelance editing services, his teaching, and his professional illustration and design work at www.jeffgerke.com.

Finally, if you'd like to see some of Jeff's own fiction, the first novel in Jeff's military thriller trilogy is free. Search for *Operation: Firebrand—Origin* on Amazon.

To whet your appetite (and show that he uses the material in *Hack Your Reader's Brain* in his own fiction, here are the first 10 pages of *Operation: Firebrand—Origin.*

Operation: Firebrand—Origin

Part 1: Death of a Navy SEAL

Today I am going to kill a man in cold blood.
The thought felt wrong in Jason Kromer's mind, like a rock in the heel of his boot.

He watched the thick Indonesian jungle glide by the side of the Mark V Special Operations Craft as it purred upstream toward the insertion zone. Gasoline and engine exhaust mixed with the stink of the river mud churned up beneath them. The soldier's fingers slid down the smooth barrel of the sniper rifle in his lap. It had a camouflage polymer stock. Perfect for killing from a distance, in hiding.

Jason could see Lieutenant Stemper forward, in the boat's cabin, talking on the satellite radio. He paused from penciling coordinates and glanced back at Jason, his sun-bleached eyebrows bunched. Then he turned away and signed off. Stemper called Doug "Chimp" Bigelow and Tom Sikes over to him. Chimp was Jason's spotter in the sniper team; Sikes was First Squad's radioman. The three of them walked aft to Jason,

Jason felt like standing and saluting, despite all his years of SEAL conditioning against the trappings of traditional military protocol. He managed to restrain himself.

"Well, it's confirmed, you lucky dogs," Stemper said. "Looks like we're going to get ourselves some real action today after all."

Oh, great.

Bigelow's wide face and prominent ears turned to Jason and Sikes and then back to Stemper. "Hoo-yah, baby." He shook Jason's shoulder until they were both grinning like idiots. "Gonna party today!"

The other four members of First Squad, Foxtrot Platoon, SEAL Team Three, scooted into earshot. The boat's crewmen were close, too, but managed to at least appear not to be eavesdropping.

"What's the op, sir?" Jason asked.

"Target of opportunity," Stemper said. "Intel boys have been flying one of them remote model airplane drones right around here, and they think they got themselves a real bad boy. Back in—" He noticed the others crowding around and gestured to Jason, Bigelow, and Sikes. "You boys mind if they listen in?"

"No problem, sir," Sikes said.

"All right, then, gather 'round, children, and I'll tell you a bedtime story."

The SEALs came forward, along with members of the boat's crew. A few grinned enviously at Jason and Bigelow and Sikes.

"As you boys remember," Stemper said, "back in the early nineties there was some really bad action over in East Timor, just a few hundred miles that way." He pointed southeast. "Massacres, soldiers firing on peaceful demonstrators, rapes. All that. Things have pretty much died down thanks to us being here, among other things. But there's still bad blood. Lots of the military thugs behind those crimes were never caught.

"Well, the intel boys think they've located one of the worst. Muslim extremist militiaman named Amien Dewantoro. One of the leading triggermen behind the Dili massacre. As I was telling our lucky fire team here, one of those radio control recon drones has pinpointed Dewantoro right here in our backyard. Local informants tipped intel off that he was coming out of hiding to see the family. The locals don't think the target will stay put for more than a few hours, so it's up to us four to go in and take him out."

Jason, Bigelow, and Sikes accepted the hand slaps and mock punches from the team.

"Now you see why I always make you two lug that Remington and spotter scope wherever we go, don't you, boys?" Stemper said to Jason and Bigelow.

"Yes, sir."

"You never know when you're going to get asked to the dance." Stemper turned to the group. "Kromer and Chimp Bigelow will be the sniper pair; Sikes will be handler for the guide; and I'll go to be sure everybody keeps their heads down."

He handed a color printout to Jason. It was a blurry photo of a brown-skinned militiaman holding a Russian-made assault rifle over his head in victory. "Here's our guy. You boys take a good look at that face because we'll have to ID him in the field. Kromer, I want you to hang onto that for the op. All right, the rest of you apes clear outta here. Everything else is just for my sweethearts."

The group dispersed.

Jason stared at the photo of the man he was going to kill. How many times he'd longed for an op like this. But now . . . ?

Stemper brought his team of three close. "Here's the deal, boys: This ain't just your usual assassination."

Jason leaned forward with the others. Stemper was barely whispering.

"See, we're not supposed to be conducting any combat activities," Stemper. "Just little recon patrols like we did today. But . . ."

He looked over his shoulder, as if one of the river crocodiles might've slithered onto the deck.

"But, you see, the East Timor honchos want this guy bad. And it seems that Washington wants to do them a favor." He looked intently at each one of them. "So, no mistakes."

Jason tried to read Stemper's expression. "Are you telling us what I think you're telling us?"

"Absolutely."

Bigelow looked at Jason. "You ever been on a black op before, Jace?"

"No, I haven't, Chimp. Have you, Sikes?"

"Not unless you're referring to my date last month with Miss Ophelia Johnson."

They traded high-fives. Jason and Bigelow did the hand jive handshake they'd worked out in BUD/S training.

"Yeah, yeah," Stemper said, "you think it's a good thing. But I'm here to tell you it ain't all that great. We'll never be able to tell anyone about it. We'll never win a medal for it. And . . . *and* . . . if we get into trouble out there, we're pretty much on our own. The Navy's not going to scramble an F-18 to save our necks, and I guarantee the Army's not going to flush an Apache to give close cover, not for a mission that isn't supposed to be happening. You understand me?"

"Yes, sir."

"Gosh, sir," Bigelow said, "when you talk like that I get all excited."

"Well, stow it, mister. I want you sharper than my ex-wife's tongue when we get off this boat." Stemper waved a mosquito from his ear and took a notepad out of his chest pocket. "Here's our GPS coordinates. Get out your maps. We're putting in where the local guide is. That's about fifteen minutes away, so listen up."

Five minutes later the briefing was over and Stemper moved forward in the boat.

Sikes followed him. "I'm not too sure about your sniper team, Lieutenant," he said in a faux whisper that was loud enough for the long-legged waterbird wading near the shoreline to hear.

"What are you talking about, Sikes?"

"Well, just look at them. Neither one's in his ghillie suit. They don't have a really long-range rifle between them. And Bigelow's got those big ol' flappy ears. I'm just afraid they're not up to the job."

"Well, what would you suggest, Sikes?" Stemper said.

"I don't know, sir. I was thinking we'd have a better chance of operational success if we gave the sniper rifle to those orangutans we saw this morning."

That brought a chorus of simian sound effects from the peanut gallery.

"Plus," Sikes said, all humor gone from his voice, "I just don't think Kromer has the chutzpa to pull the trigger. Not with his WWJD bracelet on and all."

Instantly the appraising look returned to Stemper's eyes as he looked at Jason.

Jason felt his face flushing.

Finally, Stemper slapped Sikes on the back of the head. "You just worry about getting yourself ready, Sikes."

"All right, partner," Bigelow said to Jason. "I'm gonna go prep. See you in ten."

Jason nodded and turned his attention to the .308 Remington Model 700 rifle. His murder weapon.

Operation: Firebrand—Origin is available at Amazon.com.

28735926R00044

Printed in Great Britain
by Amazon